THREE QUEENS
ONE MAGNIFICENT CITY

Contents

ISBN: 978-1-910335-24-6

First published in 2015 by Trinity Mirror

and

Liverpool City Council
Municipal Buildings
Dale Street
Liverpool L2 2DH

Printed and bound in the UK by Buxton Press

Mayor of Liverpool welcome

For seven weeks Liverpool embarked on an epic and unforgettable journey. In 2011 we were approached by Cunard with a question, and an idea began to formulate which would result in history being made on the magnificent Mersey. The question was simple – can three Cunard ships fit on the Mersey at the same time? And now we know the answer!

Right from the beginning we knew that this event alone would be monumental for the city. Liverpool is Cunard's spiritual home and the meeting of the Three Queens would give us the opportunity to celebrate this relationship, showcasing our pride in the world famous cruise line and at the same time Cunard could demonstrate their pride in Liverpool.

For most cities, one Cunard event of this scale is quite enough. But not for Liverpool. In another nod to the cruise line's 175th anniversary, Queen Mary 2 was to make another appearance on Saturday 4 July, recreating the original voyage of the first ever passenger ship Britannia.

We knew that as a city we not only had to make the most of these major events, but we wanted to make sure people engaged and connected with them. And so One Magnificent City was born.

This seven-week programme of events was a celebration of Liverpool and its transatlantic links. Kicked off by the ever popular LightNight in May, it was a pleasure to see arts and cultural organisations work together to develop a series of activities which took place across the city. From plays and photography exhibits, right through to walking tours and pop-up restaurants, it was a diverse and fascinating offer which attracted thousands of people.

And as popular and unique as the smaller events were, we

wanted to maintain our reputation for staging world-class, free events with large-scale appeal that result not only in a huge boost to the local and regional economy but also engender pride in residents and visitors.

One Magnificent City saw Liverpool host three major events in a short space of time – Three Queens, the International Mersey River Festival and Transatlantic 175. For those seven weeks, the city was on a high – there was a real appetite when it came to celebrating the city's past, present and future, and with an audience turn-out of more than 1.6million people, it was without a doubt hugely successful.

It couldn't have been more fitting for this to be called One Magnificent City. I am immensely proud to be Mayor of a city that values its heritage, and excels when it comes to marking it in style.

Joe Anderson, Mayor of Liverpool

Honoured to celebrate a special anniversary with a special city

They say home is where the heart is. Well, Liverpool and its people certainly opened their hearts to Cunard in May and July 2015 – just as they have always done.

Liverpool's 'daughter' came home to celebrate 175 years of history. A history shared by one magnificent city and a company that has simply become the most famous name in shipping. And what a way to highlight that special relationship!

The Liverpool events were staggering both in their scale and uniqueness, and because everything went so smoothly, I am sure anyone attending will have assumed that these were relatively simple events to organise.

However, nothing that took place could have happened without the hard work and close collaboration of all the people involved from across the city and wider region over several years. Those developed relationships are perhaps the most important thing I will treasure from my 175 experience.

During the three-day celebration, 1.2 million people turned out on 25 May to see the three biggest ever Cunard ships salute our birthplace. It was a salute the like of which has never been seen and maybe, just maybe, will never be seen again. Even the Red Arrows got in on the act!

And thousands greeted the arrival and celebrated the departure of Queen Mary 2 on 4 July, on the actual anniversary of the first Cunard departure from the Mersey, after the most uplifting concert to mark our anniversary took place at the Anglican Cathedral.

The pages of this book proudly remind us of spectacles so magnificent they will ensure the Cunard name will remain as revered in our 'spiritual home' for the next hundred or so years as it has for the last 175 years!

Angus Struthers, Director, Cunard

Seven magnificent weeks Liverpool can be proud of

There is rarely an events season that goes by when this city does not make me massively proud in one way or another. Culture is the beating heart of this city, and although references are frequently made to the 'heyday' of our huge European Capital of Culture success, I think 2015 has proved beyond doubt, we do not need a title to be a cultural capital. It would have been an easier option to focus our attentions on the two Cunard visits and just make an event of these beautiful vessels on the Mersey. But that is not Liverpool's style.

We saw an opportunity for a culture-packed seven weeks and we grabbed it with both hands – and I really do not think there are many, if indeed any, other cities who would have the ambition and tenacity to do this. But it is not something Culture Liverpool could have achieved on its own. Liverpool has a thriving cultural scene and behind this are dozens of small and large organisations working relentlessly to place culture at the heart of everything they do. When we approached them with our vision for 2015 and One Magnificent City, the enthusiasm and support for the proposal was overwhelming.

Immediately, ideas and suggestions began to germinate and within an incredibly short period of time we had the makings of a stellar events programme which would excite, educate and invigorate a wide audience.

Yes, we wanted to celebrate Cunard and its relationship with its spiritual home, but we also wanted to explore the wider impact of transatlantic travel on the city, and shine a spotlight on the influences that travelled across the Atlantic including food, fashion and music. And with such a diverse and enthralling series of activities taking place across the seven weeks, this was achieved.

I would like to take this opportunity to thank everyone who was involved with One Magnificent City - from the arts organisations who went above and beyond to make this a stand-out programme, Arts Council England and the city's businesses who supported each event, right through to Cunard who brought their majestic vessels to the River Mersey and, of course, the hundreds of thousands of people who came to Liverpool to be part of this unforgettable period in the city's history.

We are a magnificent city, and they were seven magnificent weeks that showed the world exactly what this beautiful, inspiring city can do.

Claire McColgan, Director, Culture Liverpool

14

Celebrations underway as first Cunard Queen sails into sight

Alarm clocks went off bright and early for those eager to catch the first glimpse of Queen Mary 2 sailing into the Mersey. The iconic ship was first sighted off the Sefton coastline by those huddled under umbrellas on the Crosby promenade at about 6.20am.

Sightings in New Brighton soon followed as crowds lined both sides **of the river** despite the drizzly conditions. The weather began to **improve as the m**agnificent vessel gradually made its way to the Pier **Head. Passengers be**lted out The Beatles classic *Hey Jude* at the top **of their voices as the ship,** the first of the Three Queens to arrive in **Liverpool, began to dock at** around 9am.

On board, Lord Mayor of Liverpool Erica Kemp presented Cunard with the Freedom Roll of Association, the highest honour the city can bestow, in recognition of the company's "proud association with Liverpool dating back to its inception".

Crowds continued to flock to the waterfront throughout the day, with an estimated 50,000 having visited the Pier Head by 6.30pm. Thousands more gathered near the Three Graces later in the evening to watch the Amazing Graces light show, taking place on three consecutive nights.

The dazzling projections beamed onto the Royal Liver Building, the Cunard Building and the Port of Liverpool Building explored Liverpool's shipping heritage and was followed by a spectacular mid-river fireworks display at 10.30pm.

It concluded a memorable first day to the weekend's celebrations, with the main event to come in a few hours' time when Queen Elizabeth and Queen Victoria would join their sister ship for a very special homecoming on the River Mersey.

Three Queens reunited as a city rejoices their homecoming

The remarkable homecoming of the Three Queens was not only one of the most important moments in maritime history, but among the most eagerly awaited, too. So it was no surprise when spectators started arriving at the Mersey waterfront in large numbers several hours before the 'river ballet' spectacular.

Queen Mary 2 set off from the cruise terminal at 10.45am and headed for the mouth of the river to greet her sister ships, Queen Elizabeth and Queen Victoria, which had sailed in from Orkney and Guernsey. Folk classic *The Leaving Of Liverpool* rang out across the water, followed by Rod Stewart's *Sailing*, while performances from the Band of the Royal Marines, Liverpool Welsh Choral and city soprano Danielle Thomas on the steps of the Cunard Building entertained the crowds temporarily left behind.

Over at Seaforth, there was hushed anticipation on board Queen Mary 2 as her sister ships appeared out of the gloom, followed by excitement as the vessels passed by. They were being closely monitored by Liverpool Cruise Terminal manager Angie Redhead, who kept in regular contact with the ships' pilots to ensure everything went as planned.

The Queens moved into formation – Elizabeth at the head and Mary at the stern, with Victoria between the two – and then glided slowly up the Mersey towards the city.

More than a million people gathered to watch the magnificent occasion unfold, with crowds reported to be 30 deep in some places. They looked on in awe as tug boats sprayed a giant V of water in front and behind the convoy, and each ship was greeted with a gun salute by 103 Regiment 208 Battery Royal Artillery as they reached the Cunard Building.

>

The ships responded with a long, low sounding of their horns, which echoed across the city as they took up their positions between the Pier Head and the Echo Arena. The sun shone as they then performed a 360-degree turn, again sounding their horns, in a magnificent salute to their spiritual home.

The Red Arrows then streaked overhead, trailing their trademark red, white and blue smoke behind them, and their appearance was greeted with huge cheers from the delighted guests on board each ship and on either bank of the river.

At 2.10pm, Queen Mary 2 left the city to continue her 10-day British Isles cruise, while Queen Elizabeth berthed at Liverpool Cruise Terminal and Queen Victoria anchored in the middle of the Mersey.

Later that afternoon, at Liverpool Parish Church, the links between the city and Cunard were celebrated. The event was also a commemoration for Cunard's Atlantic Conveyor container ship, which had been attacked exactly 33 years earlier during the Falklands War. Twelve men, six of them Cunard seamen, died in the Exocet missile strike and subsequent fire.

A memorial plaque was dedicated by the Bishop of Liverpool, the Rt Rev Paul Bayes, who spoke of the close bond between the shipping giant and the city. He told the congregation: "What a weekend it's been! We've reconnected with Cunard. We have welcomed these ships to their spiritual home. Maybe after this weekend it means more than ever before?"

In the evening, thousands of people flocked to the waterfront for another stunning Amazing Graces display before waving farewell to the second of the Three Queens. At 10.30pm, fireworks lit up the sky to mark the departure of Queen Elizabeth, which set off under the stars towards Southampton. It was a spectacular conclusion to an unforgettable day.

IN REMEMBERANCE OF
THOSE WHO LOST THEIR LIVES ON
THE ATLANTIC CONVEYOR
DURING THE FALKLANDS CONFLICT
PLACED BY
LIVERPOOL JUNIOR CHAMBER
SIMULTANEOUSLY WITH
THE JUNIOR CHAMBERS OF
COVENTRY OF PLYMOUTH,

Queen Victoria's special send-off brings homecoming celebrations to a close

It was time to say a final farewell as the curtain came down on the Three Queens bank holiday spectacular. With her sister ships having already departed, Queen Victoria remained at the Liverpool waterfront for a few more hours to provide one last chance to anyone wanting a close-up view of a giant Cunarder.

Thousands of people lined Princes Parade ahead of a special musical performance to bid farewell to the final Cunard ship to leave Liverpool. The North West Area sea cadets performed a goodbye semaphore before singer Danielle Louise Thomas sang *You'll Never Walk Alone* as the ship departed Liverpool at 5pm.

There was one last surprise in store, however, as the liner delighted the crowd with a 360-degree turn while guests onboard waved union flags from the balconies of their cabins.

Queen Victoria sailed past Crosby's promenade, where many people braved strong winds to catch a final glimpse of the ship as she left the River Mersey. Among them was maritime enthusiast Fred Wilson, who was armed with binoculars for the best possible view.

"I've been into ships for a long time and what's happened in Liverpool this bank holiday weekend will make history," he said. "That probably won't ever happen again in my lifetime. It's a privilege to see."

'Transatlantic 175' weekend extends cultural celebrations

Cunard's anniversary celebrations continued long after the homecoming of the Three Queens. On 4 July, Queen Mary 2 recreated the original 1840 voyage from the Mersey to North America as part of Liverpool's 'Transatlantic 175: From Mersey to Manhattan' weekend.

It was the centrepiece of two days of cultural events which included a world record attempt for the most models on a catwalk; a giant waterfront disco; a free food festival; an extravaganza of vintage music, film, food and fashion; and a cavalcade of classic cars from both sides of the Atlantic.

Curated by Wayne Hemingway MBE, the weekend proved to be an overwhelming and spectacular success, capturing a unique sense of community and pride.

Over 200,000 people turned out for the celebrations, which began with the arrival of Queen Mary 2 at Liverpool Cruise Terminal on Saturday night. The 'Vintage on the Dock' and 'Eat the Atlantic' food festival got things underway on Saturday followed by the world record-breaking 'Very Big Catwalk', which saw 3,651 models – including thousands of members of the public – take to the runway on the Pier Head.

The evening's entertainment included the 'Very Big After Party' while a spectacular fireworks display sent Queen Mary 2 off on her anniversary transatlantic crossing. The carnival atmosphere continued on the Sunday with a 'Classic Car Cavalcade' and a 'Transatlantic Cake Fest' before a memorable and hugely successful weekend was brought to a close.

very

ROCHELLE HUMES

A seven-week spectacular Liverpool can be proud of

The homecoming of the Three Queens and Transatlantic 175 were just two of several fantastic events taking place as part of the 'One Magnificent City' celebrations. Honouring Liverpool's internationally renowned maritime history and transatlantic links, the seven-week programme proved hugely popular, attracting over 1.6 million visitors to the city.

Launched on Friday 15 May with LightNight – a one-night arts festival offering a vibrant mix of light projections, street performance, exhibitions and hands-on workshops across 50 Liverpool locations produced by Open Culture – the One Magnificent City programme culminated in Transatlantic 175 on 5 July and provided plenty of fun-filled family entertainment in between.

Other events included 'The Crossing' at Liverpool ONE, a unique 30-minute audio experience celebrating the music, fashion and culture Liverpool shares with New York; while 'Time Liners' brought to life the stories of Cunard workers in a special new installation inside the Cunard Building itself.

There was plenty more entertainment as Liverpool awaited the arrival of the Three Queens in May, and when they departed after the three-day waterfront spectacular, the celebrations continued with Sound City, the annual 'International Mersey River Festival' and the 'Rock 'n' Roll Marathon'.

Afterwards, Mayor of Liverpool, Joe Anderson, said:
"The achievements of those seven weeks were astounding. When it comes to events, the ambitions of this city are unrivalled. With a programme of challenging and mostly free activities, Liverpool has without a doubt raised the bar."

Acknowledgements

Liverpool City Council and Cunard would like to extend a big thank you to all our funders and sponsors without whose support and encouragement none of these events would have been possible.

On behalf of all who read this book, a heartfelt thank you goes to all the photographers for their stunning images, without which, this book would not exist.

Thanks to our professional photographers Ant Clausen, Mark McNulty, Pete Carr and Terry Bouch – commissioned by Liverpool City Council.

Thanks also to Cunard's official photographers and all our contributing photographers – Alan Edwards, Andrew Teebay, Andy Hughes, Barry Bryce, Carl Yeates, Clare McNicol, Colin Lane, David Humphreys, Gareth Jones, Gavin Trafford, Gren Atherton, Ian Cooper, James Maloney, Jason Roberts, Karen Dutton, Katie Condron, Lynda Husband, Niall Lea, Open Culture, Phil Hogan, Sheila Powell, Simon Purcell, Sound City, The Red Arrows, Tommy Wong.

For further information on events in Liverpool, follow Culture Liverpool via:

🌐 cultureliverpool.co.uk

f facebook.com/cultureliverpool

🐦 @Culturelpool

📌 Culture Liverpool

📷 Culture_Liverpool

▶ Re-live the excitement of One Magnificent City on the official Culture Liverpool YouTube channel at www.youtube.com/c/CultureLiverpool

Mayor of Liverpool

CUNARD
175

ONE MAGNIFICENT CITY
15 MAY - 5 JULY 2015
LIVERPOOL